@LOVENILOUFAR

HOLDING WATER

holding water.
@loveniloufar

ISBN: 978-1-7343867-0-7 (paperback)
          978-1-7343867-1-4 (ebook)

cover illustration by niloufar

the truth lay where the lie couldn't
attempts to keep it up
but my heart wouldn't
tried swallowing it whole
but my tongue pushed it out
secrets spilling onto the counter
damn,
forgot to buy paper towels
tried to wipe it up with my bare hands
but it dripped onto your new sneakers
leaving a stain
messing with your ego

i should've kept pretending
i should've
we were so close to the beginning
of a happy ending
instead
i sliced through the surface
with uncalculated courage
revealing that we were hollow
walls
imitating
degrading
collapsing
deflating

racing thoughts:

women do not leave good men. good men are hard to find.

faithful men are even harder

ESPECIALLY when that man is the father of her child AND he loves her AND puts up with her AND he owns a house AND has a good job AND good credit.

women do not leave good men.

ESPECIALLY when that man looks good on paper. men who look good on paper make other women jealous.

other women are a woman's greatest competition.

it's been a long long long time since
i drank this much
had no business smoking that weed with him
and that guy from dubai
in the penthouse suite in D.C. above the LV store
been practicing celibacy
and recently gave my life to Christ
broke up with my man a couple weeks ago
he thinks i've been out sleeping with a rich dude
when actually/pathetically/desperately
he is younger than me, has a huge dick, but broke

i know he is big because i've willingly managed to take off this jumpsuit that
i just bought for $15.00 looking sexy as hell in the mirror i take off my panties
and bra and face down into his bed mascara smeared onto his pillow i don't
even know what i'm thinking about he's

pushing it up in me
whispering in my ear his desire for me
made me love me temporarily
and it's been too long since
someone admired how wet i get
how tight i am
he came
went down
ate me out
orgasm
all in his mouth

laid beside me to my right looking me in my eyes
asking me how i felt

i ran to the restroom
threw up for 45 minutes

dip my head in holy water
yes, i've failed and i've faltered
now i'm your greatest example of a hypocrite
and when people tell you to trust God
i'm the excuse you use to dismiss him
hating me
you feel like i lied to you
haven't had sex in months
thinking i got tired of you
been reading my bible now
you tried to respect it
i'm sorry you were so used to having me as you wanted me and suddenly
drastically
i decided to neglect it

that was the first time i ever saw you cry
when you asked me
and i told you the truth
i started sleeping with him
while i was still living with you
even though we both were clear
i was leaving you
disrespectful
i was still living with you
how could i do that to you
so soon?

it took me four years to get that kind of emotional response
a tremble with your mouth
you asked me if i was finally happy
to get what i want?

it began in the night when i could no longer sleep next to you
because i was wishing i could be sleeping next to someone else
his hands were bigger than yours
so they had a way of making me feel smaller
more feminine
sexier and delicate

it had been some time since i heard you call me beautiful
i think you took me for granted
felt like you took advantage

so when i ended up having sex with him and you found out about it i couldn't
tell if you were hurt or if you were simply embarrassed at the thought of what
you'd have to explain to your friends

did i break your heart
or your ego?

please note
this behavior of mine
this irrational behavior of mine
was unintentional

he had a way about him, one simple very specific way about him
he was able to give me that one thing
that one thing i was missing
needing from
you

and that one thing began to magnify
obsessed over the lack of it
my emptiness began to grow
sliding down the slippery slope
i used him to fill me up

so i let him fuck me to cope

i always felt like a stranger in that house
mentally my bags packed in the corner of the garage
my threats fell short and empty
until the day it wasn't a threat anymore
battling for months
prior to us moving in together
i told you that a stable home required a foundation
and we seemed to be built on sand
my feet at the edge of the shore
i kept walking towards the waves
telling myself one day
you'd notice me
and we could be saved

i kept walking, running
as you stared at the horizon
which was suddenly above me
and i fell into the ocean

drowning

drowning at the bottom
staring up towards the sky
i could see a glimpse of the sun
a dim bulb muffled by the water
oxygen escaping me
i laid there watching God

it had been a couple of years since i seen her
she was back at her mother's house where her daughters lived
now 9 and 11
they've been living here since they were 1 and 3

this time she returned with her entire right leg shattered after being jumped
needle marks all in the crevices of her body
proper veins
her face aged, eyebrows embarrassing, missing teeth, hair ratted like she'd
soon become one of those random white people with a big nasty dread
making a statement against societal norms

i knew she'd be gone again
but while we sat on the light grey steps of the front porch where we grew up
as children
she was my best friend again
and i'm telling her about my baby daddy and how he takes me for granted

how ungrateful and stupid he is
i mean girl, foreal
i had a whole baby and came out clean with no stretch marks
barely gaining weight
i'm smart, funny, learning how to cook
i mean, i am like mother of the fucking year
and he's struggling to say thank you?
no thanks, not even a thx

been there for his daughter
planning weekends while he's working (sleeping)
no time to myself
postpartum depressed and postpartum stress disorder
preeclampsia almost had me dead at delivery
he knows i got ptsd
we've been at war, but he can't fight for me?
he just fights with me

i tell him i'm going to leave
he tells me to do what i want to do
so why don't you?
she asks me

like he said, why don't you do what you want to do?
why are you so insecure though?
automatically i wondered why i was crucifying him to an addict who never
did anything for her own damn kids
questioning my sanity because if i compared him to her he was magnificent
in his deeds
thrown off by her audacity to ask me about my insecurities when she looked
like an insecurity!
sucks teeth

who did she think she was?

i remember the day she brought me chipotle
we were both pregnant at 18
i just had my abortion but she couldn't go through with hers

she knew me
she knew on that front porch with the light grey steps
who my father was and how he was a gambling addict
pathological liar and con-artist who had a knack for stealing

we both knew how close i had been to becoming her
and in many ways
i was her

but unlike her

i could hide it underneath my skin

letter on the counter:

all you had to do was wake up early.

ALL YOU HAD TO DO WAS WAKE UP!

take care of our almost 2-year old so that i could go to starbucks and write. we've been through this. we discussed this. YOU AGREED. you were going to support me the way i have been supporting you. we are supposed to be a team. REMEMBER? you had to be at work by 11:00 am, so you were going to leave at 10:00 am, but you were to get up at 7:00 am to give me at least three hours to myself because you weren't going to be back until sunday night. REMEMBER?! i've got dreams too. i work just like you work. full time. but i don't get two days out of the week off like you do while our son is in daycare to have some time to catch MY breath, to free MY mind, and do whatever the hell else I AM trying to accomplish. waking up and putting him next to you while you snore. convincing yourself he is safe all because you gave him your phone and locked the door. you go back to sleep while he is awake. i can't trust you. i can't trust you to do the things you promised me you would do. oh, you're tired? every mother fucker in the world is tired!

I CANNOT DO THIS ANYMORE.

after six months of dating your actions changed drastically
wondered if it was all an act for me
you said i was that girl you always imagined to be with
you remembered our conversations from the 6th grade

you thought of what it'd be like to take care of me
and that's why you were here pursuing me, to take care of me
the sound of that sentence, i remember
the sweet sound of that sentence
your willingness (it seemed)
to take on such a task

i always wanted someone who wanted to shield and protect me
it had been a rough 26 years of defending myself

granted, i never thought it would be you
when we stumbled back into one another's lives
we both agreed that individually, in our own common ground
we didn't have much in common

we even stated on that day
in june
declaring it

i was going to be too much
and you'd never be enough

speaking it into existence

our first christmas
it had been eight months
two months after you took your mask off
two months after i started searching for who i thought you were
contemplating leaving you

but how do i leave something i've already lost?

lost the romance in the guy who would walk me up to the 4th floor
all 55 steps just to kiss me goodnight
your cousin's wife warned me
telling me about the honeymoon phase
guess i should've heard her with ears wide open
guess i didn't expect or couldn't accept that after multiple conversations
you'd never really go back to who you seemed to be
i always felt like you tricked me

but my friends, my dear friends, who were more skilled in long term commitments
would tell me how this was just me
doing the thing that i do when i start to get scared
when someone truly loves me
doing the thing that i do when i become afraid
not feeling worthy so i runaway

having no evidence
no way of proving them wrong
no concrete reason to leave

i stayed

the devil caught us in the details
guess we weren't strong, he caused us to fail
we weren't always like this
you used to capture me through your lens
a love for exploration and laughter
i could go anywhere with you
i could do anything with you
walks and talks at midnight in the summertime
a warm fantasy
destroyed by a burning reality

guessing best friends doesn't mean great life partners
and maybe we stretched something that was meant to be temporary
but i felt like i loved you
despite our red flags

in ways you were so patient, you were so kind, calm, and put together
nothing could sway you or pull you out of character

except that one night when i made you so angry
you began throwing shit and punching walls
screaming, you violently questioned
if this is this what i needed?

when i said i needed someone to show me love
was this what i believed love to look like?

you already began to look unfamiliar
i knew that night i had to leave before you became unrecognizable
i never wanted to hate you
we can't force each other to be something to each other just for the sake of
saying we are something to one another

although i'd love to blame you
and pull apart every intricate lie i feel you told me
return back every dream i believe you sold me
i know i contributed to this mess

we both became a mirror of one another's reflections and deep resentments
unhealthy communications and misconceptions
speaking the same language but coming out with extremely different
interpretations
of the same sentences
arguing over syntax and punctuation
why can't you understand what i'm saying?
sick of explaining that love is an action not just a word
you get on my damn nerves

did you love me to love me or
did you love me to prove something to yourself?

did i love you to love you or
did i love you to prove something to myself?

i tried to tell you what i thought i wanted
arrogant you gave me what you thought i needed
we both ended up defeated
but the truth is

i had no idea what i was looking for
because i had never taken the time
to figure it out

a string of lovers before you
but never willing to tie the knot
couldn't even tell you if this was something i wanted
or not

was i resistant to love
or simply resistant to us?

is it supposed to be this confusing?
this complicated?

you were a good man
but you weren't good for me
i saw how i was destroying you
so i had to let you be
no matter how hard you tried
you could never make me happy
because joy would never be found in you
first i had to find the peace in me
tried to cover up my insecurities
by dissecting your deficiencies
it was easier to hate you
easier to tear you apart
and fault you for not being
who i secretly wanted to be
but could never seem to achieve
my projections on you came easily
easier to analyze you
as opposed to admitting
that i did not like me
how could i love me
and if i could not love me...

racing thoughts:

A MAN CANNOT SAVE YOU! you may know this when you declare it rationally, but ask yourself if you know this subconsciously? know this in your intentions? in the actions you take? on a daily basis in your interactions? are you reactive to his behavior? are you expecting a savior? are you waiting or always the one initiating only to be left disappointed? do not use what he lacks as your excuse to not do what you need to do for you. he is not your scapegoat. claiming you're being so self-sacrificial. who is trying to save who? do you think if you save him then one day he can come around and save you? you need to become an active participant in your own rescue.

they say to "love yourself"
well let me just say it was going to take more than solo spa days
and solo dinner dates and all that
other bullshit we call self-care
to repair my internal damage
i had a knack for using men as a drug
and i've never been sober enough to manage
all of my daddy issues, mommy issues
drama trauma history
the need to be acknowledged and approved
a lack of identity
so i'd find it
in him, her, and you
oh, you love me?
i need a lot of reassurance and proof
are you sure?
i mean i think i'm so fucked up
i mean why would you?
how could you?
i did not know me
they say to be yourself
well let me just say
it was going to take
a lot more than positive affirmations
and self-help to understand
who i am and the things i've been dealt

(transition)

a new space without his face
without my mother, brother, sister
without my demons and memories
a fresh space
new closets
marble counters, deep sink, garden bathtub
two bedrooms
my own and for my son
out of my budget but somehow God is blessing me with the income
undeserving but filled with gratitude
my baby wasn't there the first night
he stayed, slept at what was now his bedroom at his father's house
but shout out to my family who
showed up with that big truck
to help me move all of my stuff
and my best friend who unpacked everything of mine
completely moved me in the first night
even had my pads and tampons organized
came through with some weed, jack and coke
i don't typically smoke
but fuck it
two tears in a bucket

sun rising

i laid on the couch
on my new couch
purchased at a discount
i did not have a bed yet

the sun rose
i stared into the space of my surroundings
i felt uncomfortable
overwhelmed

by the opportunity of peace

i carried him up the 59 steps
his little hands on my face
it was wednesday
i hadn't seen him since sunday
he was two years and two months old
my heart pounded as i put him down
unlocking the door
he pushed it open
a familiar coffee table but a new couch
his big brown eyes looked around
there were items he's seen before
but they were resting on new ground
he explored and found
his crib, with his dresser, his closet, and his clothes

i cooked the way i normally would
held him on my left hip
33 pounds as best i could
and tried to tell him
this was mommy's house now
mommy and antonio's house now
curious
he repeated with an innocence
giving me the slight hope, he understood with acceptance
i bathed him, dressed him, read to him, and held him
took his hand and walked him to his bed
until he ran

to the front door, his hand
attempting to unlock it
barely reaching the knob
"go home mommy, i want go home now mommy"
falling to my knees we were now the same height
lightly resting my chin on his small shoulder
holding tears back with strong resistance
this is home, i tried repeating with an innocence
giving me the slight hope
of my own acceptance

this decision, this choice
was the most difficult choice of my life
knowing i am the one who chose to no longer try
and remedy a relationship for the sake of my son
there is a lot of guilt
a lot of blame
a lot of misunderstanding
impatient for the day
when i no longer feel the need to explain
fearful of the long-term consequences
but either way
i would've been fearful of the consequences if i stayed
i couldn't lay in that bed anymore counting down days for his eighti-
eth birthday
it's painful to hear my son make the distinction between
his mother's house
his father's house
which one becomes his home?

a new year
2019
february came
turned 31
#thirtywon

my life being nothing as i imagined it would become
since i was eight i had big dreams
busting out the seams
life can't be what it seems
thought i'd be part of a different scene
a writer

i was supposed to be a writer by now, you know?
my name known, you know?
a woman like rupi kaur
where is all the sun and my flowers?
feeling more like a dead garden
rotten milk and no honey
i was in 4th grade when i wrote
my first poem titled *true friends*
and had the guts to ask ms. carlin
if i could read it to my class
in the 5th grade
i was able to explain *dream deferred*
ahead of my time
ms. andrews said i was gifted
the irony—

never thought i'd be the poem
and actually live it

i remember when i'd drink
i'd get drunk
i'd smoke
i'd get high
i didn't want to feel my face
chasing boys helped me escape
and now it's years later
and i'm out with my girlfriends
trying to get over this lustful attachment to the dude with a monster dick
the big ones always get me where it hurts
and i'm eating gummies and drinking patron
super sexy in an oversize white sweater, red lip, no pants, black boots
play me some drake
play me some nice for what
play it for me and let me not give no fucks
allow me to feel like i did in 2010 when they played fancy at club
play in miami
i fell asleep poolside
until i woke up with the sunrise
walked down to the beach
passed out
face down in the sand

damn, take me back to 2005
summertime
first love of my life
more like lust of my life
sex in the green corolla
up for hours in conversations
he became my best friend
i'd start the sentences he knew how to end, but
we were reckless
that halloween night intoxicated found us in college park
inside somebody's garage
sex on top of their red car
too much too soon too fast
we were meant to break up
nothing stable to last
but we were unforgettable
neither one of us can deny that

yes, take me back to when i travelled states
had a boyfriend in 2008
said he had the biggest dick in belleville, illinois
that thing messed my bladder up
he had that midwest about him
he said he was in love with me
took me to jamaica
promised to marry me
initials on the cuffs of his tailored suits
only man in the world that was of his word
he was the dream boy for every love searching girl

except
i wasn't a love searching girl

in 2013 escaping reality
caught myself crazy on a plane to california
known him since 2007
when i met him down in hampton
tatted up with the june bug on his chest
arriving, thinking i could change my life
took to the color red and had my hair dyed
planning to write under the name ms. red
a double entendre
get it?
ms. red, misread?
i always felt misunderstood
but i thought if someone could get it
he would
found love in a hopeless place
he was so broken like me
a glamorized story of two lost souls
until he stood there, high
in a cowboy hat and boots
with red designer sunglasses from the woman's section
had me trapped in an art studio for days
wrapped blankets around me like he was molding clay
snuck out without a trace
ended up at a days inn
contemplating suicide flying back on the plane

ended up in west virginia at my father's house
ended up in therapy
therapist telling me i have ptsd
based on all my traumatic history
suggested we do cognitive processing therapy three days a week
yes, i was 14 when she sexually assaulted me
yes, i was 17 when he raped me
yes, my daddy was an addict and he betrayed me
tell me it's not my fault
it's not my fault
like matt damon in *good will hunting*
help me erase all my memories
eternal sunshine of the spotless mind
call me clementine
a fucked-up girl
looking for a peace of mind

yes, play me some drake
play me some nice for what
help me escape
take me back to the days when i didn't give a fuck
my friends are cheering me on
telling me to loosen up
just have fun
don't i remember who i used to be?
31 is still so young
#thirtywon

except who i used to be isn't me
and now i have a son
these clothes aren't fitting me properly
suffocating, take this shit off me
and this drink?
this drink isn't the antidote
and this high?
this high is all smoke
i love my friends
but my friends are wrong
i'm searching for fulfillment
not just fun

walking around my apartment
all of my secrets begin to reveal themselves
the mess on the counter
dishes needed back on the shelf
all the chaos belonging to myself
mailbox hasn't been unlocked in over a month
and this bathtub needs to be scrubbed
the need to take responsibility for my own life is apparent
i catch myself in the mirror
although a layer of dust prevents me from seeing myself clearer
i am still in my infant stages of progress
inhales of courage and exhales of caution
unraveling the depths of my subconscious
trying my best to honor the process
i take my fingers and trace them down the glass
there's no longer anybody else to blame
my reflection boldly stares back

the things
i've carried
buried
deep
in baggage
how do i
even begin
to unpack
this?

patterns of fixing people
a fixation
telling myself they are lost
they need saving
losing myself in their misbehaving
convincing myself they're my responsibility
how arrogant of me to think
i have the answers
to questions that i am still asking myself
pretending to be an angel
while i wear broken wings
saying things with false expertise
when really
it was just easier
it felt safer to invest my energy
to focus
on something
somebody
other than me but eventually,
eventually...

patterns of cheap thrills
weed, alcohol, and popping pills
hospitalization and breakdowns
a cycle of lost and found
mad woman bad woman sad woman
using the excuse of an artist
deep and profound
pleasure from my pain
hand over my mouth
learned not to make a sound
agreeing that i was crazy
how insane
i can't remember the good times
but i remember the days i lost my mind
drowning in nostalgia
around like a carousel
cries for help
demons on my chest while stuck in sleep paralysis
can't catch a break, can't catch my breath
or eyes red from insomnia
manic then spaced out
alone in a crowd
screaming out loud

patterns of my good intentions masked
by my need for approval
and random acts determined for validation
a strong desire for appreciation
disappointment in unmet expectations
chasing timelines
exchanging dreams for plans
attempts to fit in
still a tiny fire remained lit within
and every now and again
it urged me to begin

patterns of feeling shame for my sexuality
losing my virginity at thirteen
for my curiosity
feeling deserving of the assault and the rape that followed me
haunting me
exhausting me
told so many men yes
because i didn't know how to say no
an intricate complex
of dissociation
laid in bed becoming
a reenactment
except this time i'd have the power and control
and when they'd pull out
spilling their semen all over my belly
projecting their shortcomings all on me
and leaving behind their insecurities in between my thighs
i would lie
masking this as a protest against the double standard
telling myself this was a sexual act of liberation
and it was okay this time
i was okay this time
nobody hurt me this time
because i allowed the violation

i had lost all trust in myself
given all the years of my false declarations
all of my failings
and indecisive nature
deep rooted in need for perfection
a prison in self-criticism
paralyzed
by a need to apologize profusely
for living

i am used to compromising myself
keeping parts of myself hidden
to make others feel whole
feel as though i've been composed
of multiple identities
the remnants of those
who couldn't come close
wanting to be what was needed
self-sacrificial
neglecting my freedom
a tangled web i weaved
practicing to deceive
cracking open now
all those parts unknown
exposed

racing thoughts:

there is nothing to carry. aim for less distraction. more clarity. my voice is worth it. my story has purpose. can't wait on perfect. the truth is fluid. i don't need to beat myself up. and pay for my mistakes over and over and over again. i can break chains. i can be free.

despite what is said of me. despite what they say to me. i am capable.
i am able.

waiting on the journey to start when i've been on it. THIS IS THE JOURNEY. this is the process. this is what is done in the dark. the overnight success that requires years of progress. this is the test.

nobody has to witness my breakthrough in order for it to be real.

and just because i didn't put it in a caption, doesn't mean it didn't happen.

i remember when my breasts were 21 and could stand on their own
when my nudes were so fire
they didn't require as many posture adjustments
i remember my smile before gum recession
prior to the fillings to fill in the gaps
and the missing tooth on the right side of my mouth
i remember my hair
the thickness, the volume
i remember when my body count was in single digits
and when i love you
didn't sound like a lie in repetition
when falling for a man didn't feel like a stupid business decision
lack of return on my investment
i remember my passion
a need to write so deep
it wasn't a choice

in my adolescence my mother used to tell me
she never had the luxury of dreaming
with guilt, i could not relate

then one day she told me
if she could go back in time
she would become a dancer
i cried

this dream will never come true for her
at age 55, her highlight would be the place
she frequents every saturday night
with her girlfriends
then 4 am end up at ihop
laughing until the sunrise
and dropping into her bed
to wake up on a sunday afternoon
her only day off as a housekeeper

i cried because i knew
after all she's been through
these moments were enough for her
in her dance was her resilience
perseverance and her joy
her freedom from feeling jaded

i cried because i knew
a glimpse of what i could've been
could never be enough for me
so for as much as my mother i'd like to be
how can i prevent this from happening to me?

my father was a dreamer
an escape artist and addict
he had no patience
he wanted it all fast fast fast
then crash crash crash
running from the consequences
constant disappearing acts
he lived in a state of disorganized rebellion
a fuck it sense of mentality
without purpose
get rich quick schemes
you could never trust a man like him
men like him are worthless
but he was the first to ever tell me
that i was crazy to not quit my job at twenty
and risk it all
just to write
see, for as messed up as he may have been
he was convinced i had a gift
a gift for the world
he wasn't lying when he said
i am a dreamer just like him
daddy's little girl

(transition)

the other night i made dinner
a shrimp boil on a sheet pan
and i drank red wine
for the first time
it was not dinner for my son
it was not dinner for anyone, actually
i made it for me
out of curiosity
and i ate it alone
and it tasted delicious

the other morning i woke up
and drove to the lake
the water beneath a thick fog
the geese in formation to take off
they flew towards the clouds
above the morning horizon
without hesitation
without excuse

the other day i went to my favorite diner
sitting in the corner with a pen and my journal
jotting down my self-discovery
ordering the breakfast platter with my coffee
a favorite pastime of mine
watching people with close observation
wondering their life stories
wondering about their childhood dreams
how many became who they wanted to be?

the other afternoon i hugged my son
with great intention
and for the first time i felt gratitude
without resentment
towards myself

here is his little life
his lifetime spans to only three years now
and the funniest sayings come out of his mouth
how did he learn to be so brave?
jumping from the coffee table to the couch

how is he so certain in his faith?

the other week
i found myself staring out my window
sitting at my wooden table
thinking about how it was
given to me by some old woman
whose husband died
she and him had a steady life
predictable and content
he used to sit on one side
and she'd smile on the other end
but now she found herself a new man
and this old thing was getting in their way
her past was taking up their space
she'd love the closeness of his face
the warmth of his chest
so she got rid of what was good
to love on what was best
for her
for the first
time

unraveling in the process of forgiveness
without witness

gathering in the process of acceptance
without witness

without witness

racing thoughts:

healing occurs on mundane mornings where my actions feel monotonous
and predictable. waiting impatiently for a change. it occurs in the evening
when i slice through cold raw chicken breast and the knife dauntingly hits
the cutting board. healing occurs when my son has pneumonia, but doctors
refuse to diagnose him because it's not showing up in his x-rays the way it's
showing up in my intuition so in my quest for the answer i show up at the
ER three times. diligent, i begin to find reason to trust myself again. healing
occurs when there are no messages from a man in the morning, or the
evening, and the only thing wrapping itself around me is the grey and yellow
blanket my mother bought me for christmas a few years back. healing occurs
in my therapy sessions when i am challenged to question my current patterns
of thinking and beliefs. healing occurs when i don't need to have a roundtable
discussion for every decision i anticipate because i am managing to stand on
common ground with my own judgement.

healing occurs in what i often overlook. a combination of perseverance and
resilience and the audacity to believe that the way i've been living, thinking,
breathing no longer benefits me.

healing occurs without witness.

when you speak your fears out loud
their hold begins to weaken
and where there are your wounds
courage begins to seep in

practice acts of confession:

sometimes guilt swallows me up
when i look at my son, laughing
and i know that all his love isn't enough
because i still have dreams
and things
on a list of hope
requiring my attention

often i've felt inadequate
my writing immature, underdeveloped
when i compare it
to works of literature
descriptions lacking the delicacy required
to create profound poetry
i become insecure and question
my own nerve
who am i to think i could deserve
monetary acknowledgement
for my gift?
insecure, i become jealous of those accomplished
embarrassed, i turn my phone off
and throw it on the couch

shame exists still
and i work through it
reminding myself of my value
telling myself
that i am not the choices i've made
and i am not what has been done to me
however,
i cringe when my thoughts become intrusive
and i remember when i've been the villain
in control of my victim
grounding my feet into the earth
i push in to feel human
convincing myself that i am not
my trauma

and it is an internal battle
wanting to feel warmth
and connection
instead i compartmentalize
and rationalize things to death
because if i can understand the concepts
then i can tear them a part
and have more control
and less feeling

(transition)

time does not wait, nor
does it rush

i've been clearing out the mold
my insides carrying around a funk
gradually growing throughout the years
and the only way to get rid of it
was to penetrate at the root

i found her
sitting with her head bowed in a corner
i've been trying to defend her
all this time

her weight
an anchor, keeping me

please stand up

there is no way i can pretend like this anymore
with this mask on
i tell her

there is no way you can save me like this
in this stillness
i tell her

there is no way i can live like this
with these fears
i tell her

there is no way i can love like this
with these walls
i tell her

i need my son to know me better than this
without this pain
i tell her

i can't keep existing in this narrative
in this story
i tell her

i met a kind man the other day
his eyes are honest, with clarity
his truth, a rarity

i want to love him
and i want to allow him to love me

i tell her

i look at her
with a deep inhale
and great hesitation
a swallow
quick exhale
she's all i've ever known
she is familiar
and served her purpose

please, stand up
she rises

steps into my palms
she becomes liquid
my hands open
fingers apart
i watch her slip

for the first time
i do not stop her

and
i let her go

holding onto her was like
holding water.

Made in the USA
Middletown, DE
22 December 2019